Municipal Bonds – What You Need To Know to Start Earning Tax-Free Income

By Robert A. Harbeke, CFP®

Table of Contents

1 – What are municipal bonds?

You may ask, "Why should I consider investing in municipal bonds?" It goes back to the old saying, "It's not what you earn but what you keep." With municipal bonds, the interest is exempt from federal taxes and, in many cases, state and local taxes. So while you may receive a lower rate from a municipal bond, if you keep all the interest you are likely to have more left than with a taxable bond after the taxes are paid. My experience has been that as a person's net worth increases, so does their interest in municipal bonds. Their relative stability in price, safety, and attractive yield make them suitable for conservative investors.

In this book I will show you what municipal bonds are, where you can find them, how they are issued, what to look for, and some of the risks to be aware of if you own them. Those with shorter maturities are referred to as notes and longer maturities as bonds. For the purpose of this discussion, we will simplify that by calling them all bonds.

Municipal securities are debt obligations issued by various government entities to pay for what are considered essential or important purposes. Common issuers are states, cities, counties, as well as special districts and agencies. Some of the more frequent uses are to build schools, roads, hospitals, water and sewer plants, electrical generating plants, and airports. These bonds are issued by the municipality and then sold to investors, generally in $5,000 increments. Interest is paid out to the investor, generally semi-annually, which gives the issuer time to generate the revenue to pay the interest on the bonds and pay off the principal at maturity. So you are lending them money backed by their promise to pay you a stated interest rate and the principal when due.

Issuance of municipal securities dates back over 100 years. The Supreme Court ruled in 1895 that the federal government had no power under the Constitution to tax interest on municipal bonds. Later the 16th Amendment was codified in the Revenue Act of 1913 to provide for the exemption of interest on state and local bonds. (IRS Publication – Introduction to Tax-Exempt Bonds)

A simple example of a series of bonds would be as follows:

Amount	Due in Year	Rate
5,000,000	11	2.2%
5,000,000	12	2.4%
5,000,000	13	2.6%
5,000,000	14	2.8%
5,000,000	15	3.0%
5,000,000	16	3.2%
5,000,000	17	3.4%
5,000,000	18	3.6%
5,000,000	19	3.8%
5,000,000	20	4.0%
Total = $50,000,000		

In this case the issuer would pay only the interest for the first 10 years and then start paying off the principal in year 11. Each year $5,000,000 of principal would be paid along with the interest. The amount of interest paid would go down as the amount of bonds outstanding is reduced. Most bonds are issued in a series like that to match the bond maturities with the likely repayment source. This lets you as a buyer determine the maturity of bond that you would like.

2 – Types of bonds

There are two main types of municipal securities. The first is:

General Obligation Bonds

These are bonds that are backed by the full faith and credit of the issuing party. In addition to the tax supporting the bond, they have the taxing power of the city, state or county to count on. Most general obligation bonds have to be voter-approved prior to issuance. An example of a general obligation bond would be the city of Scottsdale issuing a bond for several city projects. There is not a pledge of any specific income to pay the bonds, but it is a general obligation of the city.

With its AAA rating and the taxing power of the city behind it, you can be reasonably certain that the bond will be paid.

Revenue Bonds

Revenue from the various features, whether fees, rents, tolls, or taxes, are a feature of revenue bonds. Income from the highways, bridges, airports, water and sewer projects, hospitals and housing for low- and moderate-income individuals are an example of the things that can be financed by a revenue bond. Many of the securities are issued just for this purpose. Investors are comfortable having a specific cash flow identified to pay their bonds, and the bigger the spread above what is needed, the better the risk of payment on the bonds.

An example of a revenue bond would be highway bonds where the maturities are spread out over 20 years. Each year the interest would be paid and the shortest bond paid off. The stream of revenue for the highway project is pledged to support the bonds.

3 - Bonds with special features

Insured Municipals

Many bond issuers would be without a good rating unless they had a secondary source of payment. For this reason a lot of bond issuers have insured them with a policy from a company that insures municipal bonds. Up until five years ago, having an insured bond would mean a rating of AAA.   Today most bonds trade on their own merits. Those same insurance companies have had to live with lower ratings as they didn't have sufficient money to cover major losses from 2008. As a result, the ratings of the insurance companies are no longer AAA and in some cases are below investment-grade.

Today you won't find many bonds that are insured as it doesn't mean as much as it used to. There was a period of time for a year or two after the market downturn in 2008 that some bonds were insured by Berkshire Hathaway. But they have since decided not to take on that risk so they have discontinued insuring bonds. You may be able to still find some of them.

Non-rated Municipal Bonds

Non-rated bonds are securities that do not have a rating assigned to them by one of the major rating agencies. This does not necessarily mean it is a lower quality bond as municipal bonds are not required to have a rating. A non-rated bond will generally have a higher yield than a comparably rated bond. Issuers generally have two reasons for issuing non-rated bonds. If the issue is small, it may cost more to have it rated than to pay a slightly higher rate of interest on the bond. Second, an issuer may not think the bonds will meet the rating criteria of the rating agencies and would be below investment-grade if classified.

High-Yield Bonds

High-yield municipal bonds are ones that do not qualify for an "investment-grade" rating by one of the rating agencies. In reviewing the bonds the agencies may think that there is a higher risk that the issue will not pay its obligation and then give the issuer a rating below investment-grade. High-yield municipal bonds almost always pay a higher rate of interest than investment-grade bonds to compensate investors for the credit risk they are accepting. They are volatile and speculative in nature and have increased risks compared to investment-grade bonds.

Investors should be aware of the increased risk and should find out as much as they can about the issue before investing. But by looking carefully into each bond and what backs them, you do have the opportunity to earn more interest by taking the risk to invest in them.

Callable Bonds

Many of the bonds issued today carry some type of call provision where the issuer can call all or part of the bond. Most bonds have an optional call provision where after a period of 10 years, a bond can be called in. This gives the purchaser some period of time where they are guaranteed to have the bonds. When the call provision comes up, the issuer has the right but not the obligation to redeem the bond.

Another type of call that they may have is an extraordinary call. This is where some course of action dictates when it may be called. It may be a catastrophe call or some other event where the bond may be paid off in full. It is a good idea to check on the calls and what circumstances a bond can be called as most of the bonds are potentially subject to this type of call action. This is especially true for premium bonds. If they are called early, it can affect the yield.

Defeased and Refunded Bonds

When interest rates fall below the rate of interest currently being paid by the issuer on an existing security, the issuer may want to issue new bonds to refinance the issue. In this case the issuer refunds an outstanding issue to take advantage of the new lower rate. Typically they will take the proceeds of the new issue and place them in an escrow account to pay off the older, higher-rate bonds, and most of the time, it is invested in government securities.

Then the older bonds will be called in on their earliest call date (called pre-refunded bonds), or, if non-callable, are paid at maturity (called escrow to maturity, or ETM). When this is done the bonds are defeased and are no longer an obligation of the issuer. For an investor who doesn't need the highest yield but wants the highest safety, these bonds are the highest quality.

Zero Coupon Bonds

Zero Coupon bonds are generally issued at a discount to their maturity value. They do not pay any income but pay both principal and interest at maturity, similar to a Treasury Zero Coupon bond. Because of this the rate paid is a little higher than a bond that pays semi-annually. This is ideal for those who do not need the income, or who have to have a certain sum at a given time. But if you have to sell them prior to maturity, they are more volatile in price and are more sensitive to interest rate changes.

4 – Payment history of municipal bonds

Although past performance does not guarantee future results, issuers of municipal bonds have done a good job of paying for their bonds when they are due. In addition to earning tax-free interest, when you invest in municipal bonds your major concern is getting paid back. It is important to look at the quality of the issue and assess the likelihood of getting paid back. Will Rogers is quoted as saying, "The return of your principal is more important than the return on your principal."

Issuers disclose details of their financial condition through "official statements" which are available through your financial advisor, your bank, or a library of official statements. These will help you determine the likelihood of repayment and financial strength. There are some areas of weakness in the municipal bond issuers today that you have to be careful to know what you are buying. As a general rule, it is one of the safest asset classes.

Looking back for 40 years, we find the number of defaults to be very low. The rate of default was only a little over one per year. Of all the issues rated by Moody's, only 54 municipal issues defaulted on their debt between 1970 and 2009.

Default Counts by Bond Purpose	Number of Defaults Between 1970-2009
Housing	21
Health Care	21
City, Town. County non-general obligation	4
General Obligation	3
Electric, Water or Sewer Enterprise	3
Higher Education	1
Recreation	1

Source: Moody's

Past performance is not a guarantee of future results.

5 – How Bonds are rated

Investments are generally rated by one of the rating agencies. The bonds rated by Moody's, Standard and Poor's, and Fitch, are likely to capture a higher price in the market-place. These three rate most of the bonds in the market, and those rated Baa (by Moody's) or BBB (by S&P and Fitch) or higher are considered "investment-grade," which means suitable for preservation of investment capital. While they are the best we have, we have seen them miss the mark in the days following the market weakness in 2008. Ratings should not be the sole basis for any investment decision.

Credit Ratings

Credit Quality	Moody's	Standard & Poor's	Fitch
Prime	Aaa	AA	AAA
Excellent	Aa	AA	AA
Upper Medium	A	A	A
Lower Medium	Baa	BBB	BBB
Speculative	Ba	BB	BB
Very Speculative	B, Ca	B, CCC, CC, C	B, CCC, CC, C
Default	Ca, C	D	DDD, DD, D

Information has been obtained from sources considered reliable, but its accuracy and completeness are not guaranteed.

6 - Taxable municipal bonds and Build America Bonds

Issuers will sometimes sell municipals that are subject to federal taxes. Taxable municipal bonds generally offer yields more comparable to those of other taxable bonds, such as corporate bonds or bonds issued by a U.S. governmental agency, rather than those of tax-exempt municipals.

The American Recovery and Reinvestment Act of 2009 created the new Build America Bond program. It was created to help state and local governments obtain financing for certain projects at lower borrowing costs while stimulating the economy and creating new jobs. Under this program state and local governments were permitted to issue taxable bonds in 2009 and 2010 for capital projects for infrastructure needs. The issuer would then receive a new direct federal subsidy payment from the Treasury Department for a portion of its borrowing costs equal to 35% of the total coupon interest paid to investors. The federal subsidy is treated like a federal tax rebate to the issuer; it is in no way linked to the credit quality of the issuing municipality. It is important to note that Build America Bonds are not a direct or implied line to the Treasury, nor are they backed by the U.S. government should an issuer have credit problems.

7 - How to Purchase Municipal Bonds

Municipal bonds come to market in one of two ways, either by a competitive underwriting or a negotiated offering. In a competitive underwriting a dealer, or group of dealers, offer to buy the bonds in a sealed bid at a specific time and specific date. The issuer takes the lowest cost or the best structure and awards the underwriting to the winner of the competitive bid.

I had the opportunity to represent my company in bidding on some bonds in the city where I was located. At the time and place selected, we bid on three issues, and there were about five different firms represented. The issues were a general obligation bond, a water and sewer bond, and a city street and highway revenue bond. A few minutes before 1:00 p.m., I was in contact with our home office on the structure and rates to submit. After the bids were opened, ours was the lowest average rate and we were awarded the bid. At 1:30 p.m., the bids were opened on the water and sewer bond, and we won that one as well. At 2:00 p.m., the last series on the street and highway was opened. Since we were not as interested in that issue, we didn't bid as aggressively and it was awarded to another firm. But I saw firsthand how a sealed bid process worked.

In a negotiated underwriting, the issuer chooses a dealer or group of dealers and negotiates the best deal for the interest rates and terms of the offering. Sometimes the structure of maturities is more important to the issuer than the overall cost of the bonds.

As a retail investor you can buy bonds directly on the offering in either type of offering. The dealers give preference to the retail clients in these deals as the issuers like to have local people own the bonds. The local owners tend to keep the bonds much longer, and it lets the residents of an area participate in future offerings.

Since most offerings are infrequent it is more likely that a bond being purchased by you would be a secondary position. You can go to any brokerage firm and they will likely have an inventory of bonds for their retail clients. They vary according to issuer, quality, and maturity. If this is your first purchase of a municipal bond, I would suggest you consider a bond you are familiar with, such as the city of Phoenix or Salt River Project if you live in Arizona. It is also a good idea to have in mind what maturity of bond that you are comfortable buying. If you are looking, for example, for around a 10 year holding, and they don't have any in their inventory, you can usually wait a day or two until one comes in. Their inventories are constantly changing and they will get a maturity in that you like. Or if you know the issuer you would like to have, you can ask them to look for one and they can likely find one for you.

Bonds do not generally have a commission to buy them but have what is called a dealer markup. A company may buy the bond from another dealer, mark it up, and then resell it. As a result of the continual demand for tax-exempt bonds, there is always a need for the firms to buy more bonds. If for some reason you should decide to sell your bonds, there is a ready market for them. Prices for bonds are always quoted as a percentage of face value, and the bonds are usually in $5,000 increments. A round lot is $25,000, and it is slightly easier to get a bid and a better price selling them when done in this quantity. But there is nothing wrong with buying them in $5,000 increments.

8 - Premium and Discount Bonds

When bonds are first issued, generally most of them are priced near face value. A 20-year bond may be priced to yield 4%, a 19-year bond priced to yield 3.9%, an 18-year bond priced to yield 3.8%, and so on down the line. After a few years the rates may not be close to the market rates and the prices are either at a discount or a premium to face value. Say the 20-year bond now has 15 years until it matures and the rates on a 15-year bond are 4.5%. The price on the bond would be reduced to around 92.5% of face value to make it yield 4.5%. It is paying you 0.5% less in interest for 15 years so a simple calculation would be 0.5 x 15=7.5% discount on the bond.

Similarly if the rates came down to 3.5% with 15 years left, the bond would be priced at 107.5% of face value. Using the same formula of 0.5% times 15 years would give it a premium of 7.5%. If the bond has a call provision where it can be called 10 years after issue, this would affect the price of the bond. In this case you would want to know what the yield to call would be as well as the yield to maturity. At any point in time, bonds can be equalized by price to get what is called the yield to maturity.

If you have a non-callable bond with a maturity of 10 years yielding 3%, and that is the going rate on a bond of that type, it would be priced at 100. It pays out $300 on a $10,000 bond every year, or $3000 over the 10-year period. If you could buy a 2.5% bond how much of a discount should you pay? The same $10,000 invested would pay you $2500 over the 10-year period instead of $3000. So you should pay about $500 less in this simple example. It will vary somewhat from that because of the time value of money and annual amount received, but that is how the bond market equalizes higher-and lower-rate bonds and makes them comparable to each other.

9 - Taxable Equivalent yields

Bonds can be compared to taxable bonds using another method. The way that most bonds are compared to taxable bonds is by using what are called taxable equivalent yields. Because of the tax-free nature of the municipal bonds, it

is the same as earning a higher rate
that is subject to taxation.

Example		
	4% Tax-exempt Bond	5.5% Taxable Bond
Cash Investment	$30,000	$30,000
Interest	$1200	$1650
Federal Tax	$0	$577.50
Net Return	$1200	$1072.50
After-tax Yield	4.00%	3.575%

If you invested your money in a municipal bond, you would earn $1200 in interest (a 4% yield) and pay no federal taxes. The taxable investment at 5.5% would only give you $1072.50 (a 3.575% yield) after the taxes of 35% were taken out. As you can see, the best yield is the tax-exempt yield in this case. It would be even better if you were to factor in state and local taxes. To put it another way, a 4% tax- exempt yield would be equivalent to 6.15% in a taxable bond.

Financial newspapers and business sections of major newspapers will generally list prices of widely traded municipal securities. Prices are based on $1 million lots, and prices are discounted based on larger dollar transactions. You will pay more than that based on the size of the order. You can also receive price quotes from your financial advisor. Holders of municipal bonds can sell their bonds in the secondary market. If you sell your bonds prior to maturity, you will get the market value at that point in time, which may be more or less than you paid. On the Municipal Securities Rulemaking Board-operated website EMMA, at emma.msrb.org, you can find disclosure documents, official statements, material events, and quotes.

10 – Risks

Credit Risk

Municipal bonds vary in risk depending on the issue. While they are subject to **many risks,** the **main two** are the most important. The first of these two is credit risk. This is an actual or perceived deterioration of the municipality issuing the bonds. A municipalities rating may be downgraded if the agency believes the issuer has become less able to meet its debt obligations. When a downgrade occurs, it is normally accompanied by a decline in the prices of the bonds.

When the marketplace anticipates a downgrade may be coming, price often declines before the actual downgrade. The rating agencies may also issue a "credit watch" before a downgrade, which normally brings a price decline. Or if the local economy has been particularly hard hit, you may have a default risk. If it deteriorates to this level, liquidity would be low and there may not be many bids available.

Interest Rate Risk

The second major risk is where interest rates are at. When interest rates are moving higher, bond prices will generally move lower. The opposite is true when rates are moving lower, bond prices are normally moving higher. You can think of this as a seesaw with bond prices moving in the opposite direction of interest rates. The lower the coupon rate and the longer the maturity, the more prices will move as a percentage of the amount invested. These two items, the quality of the bond and the maturity date of the bond, will be the most important in determining the price of the bonds.

Call Risk

Most bonds will be callable after a period of time, usually 10 years after they were issued. Other bonds will be non-callable for the life of the bond. When rates are lower, like they are now, bonds issued several years prior at higher rates are called in and you would lose the higher interest rate. As a practical matter, an issuer will call in a bond when it can issue a new bond at a lower rate than the existing bond.

When buying a bond in the

secondary market, it is important not to pay too much for a bond paying a higher rate. The seller should be able to quote the yield to maturity as well as the yield to call. In an environment where most bonds are at a premium to their face value, the yield to call can be very low. For example, a bond with a 4% coupon with three years until the call date would not be priced over 112 or you would have a negative return. If it were priced at 106, it would give you an approximate yield of 2% to the call.

Liquidity Risk

Liquidity risk is where an owner of a bond might not be able to sell a bond at a time or price that they choose. When a bond is "liquid", the holder is able to sell to an active group of broker dealers willing to bid on the issue. When some concerns arise, those same broker dealers either will not bid on the bonds or will reduce them drastically. This would create less liquidity, bigger spreads between bid prices and offered prices, and a chance that sellers will receive lower prices for their bonds. Characteristics that may affect a bond's liquidity include: the purpose of the bond, how well-known the name is in the marketplace, the rating, the size of the trade, and the current float in the marketplace.

Event Risk

This would be any type of change in the government entity or news item. A change in the local government, new regulations or tax law changes, adverse news items, or any other event can have a broad effect on the ability of bond issuers to pay interest and principal when due.

Economic Risk

A bond's vulnerable to downturns in the overall economy, and this presents a risk. During economic downturns, investors get nervous and may start to sell bonds they believe will have a harder time to pay the interest and principal. There could be a "flight to quality" where they are selling lower-quality bonds and buying either high-quality holdings or treasury bonds.

Reinvestment Risk

This is where you are unable to get a similar rate on the interest or principal when it is paid. We are in that situation now. Using a bond ladder to stagger the bonds would minimize the risk as only a little of the principal comes due at a particular time. If you know you want to reinvest for a few years, a zero coupon would take care of that risk.

An example of a bond ladder is where you may have bonds maturing in, say two years, four years, six years, eight years, and ten years. Generally the shorter bonds yield less and are higher in the later years. In two years when the bond comes due and you do not need the money for something else, you would invest in another 10-year bond and thus keep the ladder intact. This would also allow you to get the highest yield on that bond. By keeping a bond ladder you would be planning to keep bonds until maturity. This would minimize price risk and average a higher yield than if you consistently bought shorter maturities.

I have clients who have a variation of a bond ladder. Over a period of years they purchase bonds with a 25 or 30 year maturity. They rarely sell a bond, but are expecting to hold the bonds to maturity or their call date. When they are paid back the face value of the bond, they buy another one with a longer maturity to get the highest yield. Since they are not selling the bonds, but are waiting until they either mature or are called in, they always get the principal value paid back to them. By planning to hold them until they are paid, they can avoid the day to day fluctuations in price.

Enhancement Risk

Some issuers want to enhance the credit of their offerings by having the bonds insured. The insurance is a secondary promise to pay the interest and principal of the bond, when the primary issuer is unable to pay. The insurance company also is rated and subject to lower ratings due to financial difficulties and economic environments. A downgrade of a municipal bond insurer will increase the volatility and negatively affect the price and liquidity of any bonds insured by the company.

11 - Additional Resources

Additional information about individual municipal bonds, including municipal disclosure documents, market activity, and municipal market rules, is available from the Municipal Securities Rulemaking Board's (MSRB) online website **MSRB.org.**

Electronic Municipal Market Access information site, **emma.msrb.org** provides several market statistics, educational materials, recent official statements, and price information for municipal bond transactions.

You can also find bond market trading data at **finra.org** and **InvestinginBonds.com.**

If you have any general questions, they can be sent to rharbeke@gmail.com, and I will try to get back to you within a week.

This book doesn't cover every situation that is out there but is designed to guide you through the main points in looking at tax-free bonds. The key is to get as much information as you can and be informed on what it is you are buying. While tax laws can be changed at any time, I believe the tax advantages of municipal bonds will be around for quite some time.

Made in the USA
Charleston, SC
23 August 2013